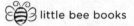 little bee books

An imprint of Bonnier Publishing USA
251 Park Avenue South, New York, NY 10010
Copyright © 2016 by Bonnier Publishing USA
All rights reserved, including the right of reproduction in whole or in part in any form.
Little Bee Books is a trademark of Bonnier Publishing USA, and associated colophon is a trademark of Bonnier Publishing USA.
Manufactured in the United States   LB 0219
ISBN 978-1-4998-0273-3 (pbk)
First Edition 10 9 8 7 6 5 4 3
ISBN 978-1-4998-0274-0 (hc)
First Edition 10 9 8 7 6 5 4 3 2 1

Library of Congress Cataloging-in-Publication Data:
Names: Ohlin, Nancy, author. | Larkum, Adam, illustrator.
Title: Blast Back! : The Titanic / by Nancy Ohlin ; illustrated by Adam Larkum.
Description: First edition. | New York, New York : Little Bee Books, [2016] |
Series: Blast back! | Includes bibliographical references.
Subjects: LCSH: Titanic (Steamship)—Juvenile literature. |
Shipwrecks—North Atlantic Ocean—Juvenile literature.
Classification: LCC G530.T6 O56 2016 | DDC 910.9163/4—dc23
LC record available at http://lccn.loc.gov/2016004447

Identifiers: LCCN 2015039047

littlebeebooks.com

BLAST BACK!

THE TITANIC

by Nancy Ohlin   illustrated by Adam Larkum

little bee books

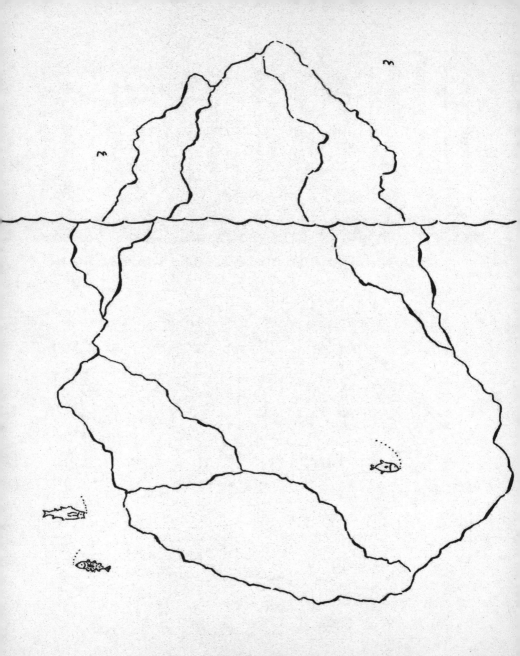

CONTENTS

9   Introduction

12   A Brief History of the *Titanic*

16   The First Ocean Liners

25   The Building of the *Titanic*

32   Preparing for the Maiden Voyage

38   The Voyage Begins

46   Life on Board

54   The First Warnings

62   The Iceberg

70   Hopeless

74   The Distress Signal

78   Saving the Passengers

84   The Sinking of the *Titanic*

92   Rescue

95   The Aftermath

100   The Discovery of the *Titanic*

110   Selected Bibliography

INTRODUCTION

Have you ever heard people mention the sinking of the *Titanic* and wondered what they were talking about? What kind of ship was it? Why did it sink? Were there any survivors? Was the sunken ship ever found?

Let's blast back in time for a little adventure and find out. . . .

A BRIEF HISTORY
OF THE *TITANIC*

The *Titanic* was a type of ship called an ocean liner. It was owned by a British shipping company called the White Star Line.

The *Titanic* left Southampton, England, on April 10, 1912, with more than two thousand people on board. It made stops in France and Ireland before starting across the Atlantic Ocean for New York City. But it never made it there. It collided with an iceberg on April 14, and sank early the next morning.

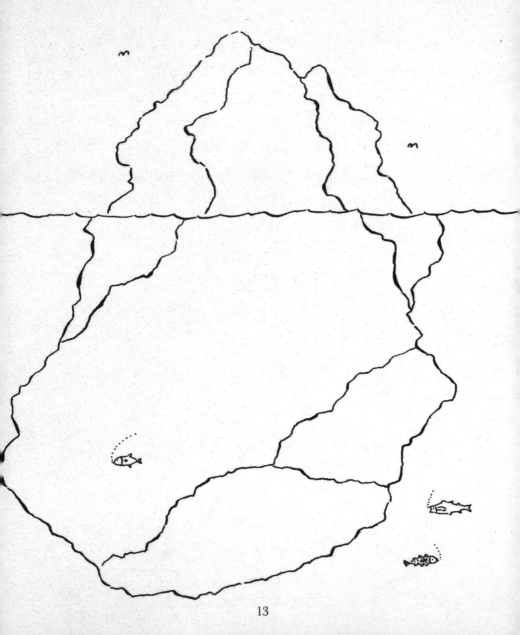

In its time, the *Titanic* was one of the largest ships in the world. Its full name was the RMS *Titanic*, or Royal Mail Ship *Titanic*, because it carried mail as well as passengers. People called it the "Millionaire's Special" because it was so luxurious. Ironically, some also called it "unsinkable" because of its safety features.

The *Titanic* tragedy is one of the most famous disasters in modern history.

THE FIRST OCEAN LINERS

Ocean liners are ships that run on a regular schedule from one seaport to another. They transport passengers, cargo, and sometimes mail, for money. The first ocean liners, in the early nineteenth century, were only a few hundred feet long. (Today the largest ocean liner is more than one thousand feet long.)

In 1839, a British businessman named Samuel Cunard, along with his partners, founded the British and North American Royal Mail Steam Packet Company. (Later it was called the Cunard Steamship Company and also the Cunard Line.) It was one of the first companies to provide year-round, regularly scheduled service across the Atlantic Ocean.

In July of 1840, the company launched its first mail steamship, the RMS *Britannia*. The *Britannia* was powered by a steam engine; it also had sails as a backup. The ship traveled from Liverpool, England, to Halifax, Nova Scotia, and then on to Boston, Massachusetts. The transatlantic crossing took only twelve and a half days.

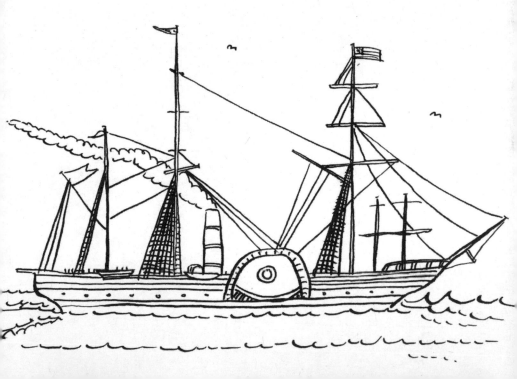

The *Britannia*'s success showed that ships could cross the Atlantic Ocean on a schedule with set departure and arrival times. Cunard went on to construct more steamship liners, so did competitors in France, Germany, the United States, and elsewhere.

By the early 1900s, the ocean liner business was booming. The airplane had been invented

in 1903 by the Wright brothers; however, there were no commercial flights (flights for paying customers) until 1914. This meant that the only way to cross the Atlantic was by boat. People wanted to travel between Europe and North America for business or pleasure. Poor Europeans wanted to immigrate to America to seek better lives for themselves and their families.

The White Star Line was one of Cunard's competitors. Founded in 1845, it had its headquarters in Liverpool, England. In 1907, Cunard introduced two new ocean liners, the *Mauretania* and *Lusitania*, which would set records for speed. Not to be outdone, White Star decided to build three ocean liners that would emphasize comfort and luxury.

These ocean liners were the *Olympic*, the *Britannic* . . . and the *Titanic*.

Do Ocean Liners Still Exist?

Ocean liners still exist; although, airplanes have all but replaced them as a mode of transoceanic travel. Probably the most famous ocean liner today is the *Queen Mary 2*, or *QM2*, which is a large, luxurious cruise ship built by the Cunard Line in 2003. (The first *Queen Mary* was retired from service in 1967 and is now a floating hotel, museum, and restaurant in Long Beach, California.)

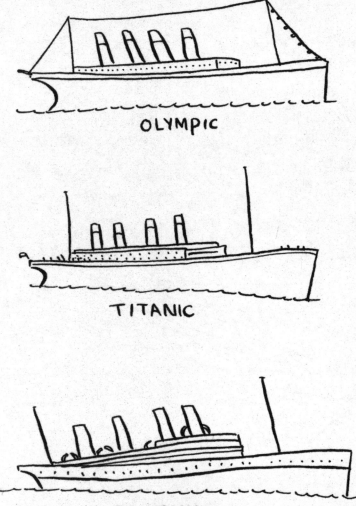

OLYMPIC

TITANIC

BRITANNIC

THE BUILDING OF
THE *TITANIC*

White Star built the *Olympic* and *Titanic* first, and the *Britannic* later. The three ships were designed and constructed by a company called Harland and Wolff. The Harland and Wolff firm was (and still is) based in Belfast, which today is the capital of Northern Ireland.

In 1909, construction began on the *Titanic*. Thomas Andrews, who was Harland and Wolff's managing director and chief of the design department, was the main designer, engineer, and shipbuilder on the project.

During the first stage, the *Titanic* was built side by side with the *Olympic* in an oversize gantry (a frame-like structure). Harland and Wolff employed around fifteen thousand people, and more than four thousand of them were involved in the construction of the *Titanic* and the *Olympic*. The workers included carpenters, welders, plumbers, painters, and many others.

Once the *Titanic*'s main superstructure and hull (the main body) were completed, the ship was launched in May of 1911. ("Launched" means that the ship was moved into the water, where the interior work could be finished.)

The *Titanic* was completed the following April.

The *Titanic* from Stem to Stern

Once completed, the *Titanic* was a floating palace that was more like a fancy hotel than a ship. Here were some of its features:

- It was 882.5 feet long. (Picture three football fields placed end to end.)

- It had nine full decks, which are like stories in a building. From top to bottom, they were called: the Boat deck; the A deck (a.k.a. the Promenade deck); the B, C, D, E, F, and G decks; and the Tank Top deck (which housed the ship's machinery). There was a partial deck at the very bottom called the Orlop deck.

- It was divided into three classes: first class (the most expensive and luxurious); second class (less expensive and luxurious, although still quite comfortable); and third class (the cheapest class). Each class had its own decks, cabins, dining areas, and other spaces.

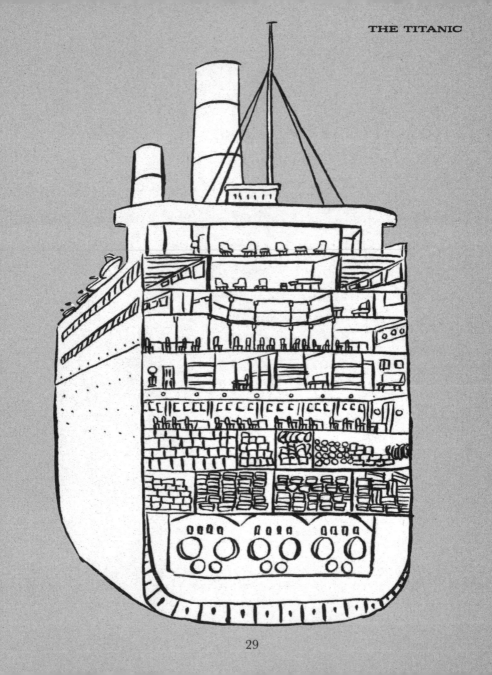

- It had a post office with five clerks and a hospital with an operating room.

- The ship's hull was made of steel; the bottom was made of extra-thick double steel.

- The hull was divided into sixteen compartments that could be closed off from one another and from the rest of the ship in case the hull was breached. The idea was that if one compartment began flooding, it could be quickly sealed off from the other compartments.

- The *Titanic* ran on three main engines that were powered by steam. Other parts of the ship were powered by steam as well, including the steering motor, refrigeration plant, heat for part of the ship, and electricity for all of the ship.

- To make all this steam, coal had to be shoveled into 162 furnaces one shovel at a time by as many workers. Around six hundred tons of coal were used every day.

- The *Titanic* had a carrying capacity of 46,328 tons, which is equal to 92,656,000 pounds.

PREPARING FOR THE MAIDEN VOYAGE

The *Titanic* had its sea trials in early April of 1912. Sea trials are tests on open water to make sure a new ship is ready for travel.

After the *Titanic* passed its sea trials, its maiden voyage was scheduled for April 10. (A maiden voyage is the first official voyage of a ship.) It would depart out of Southampton, England, with stops in Cherbourg, France, and Queenstown, Ireland. (Today, Queenstown is called Cobh.) On April 11, it would start across the Atlantic Ocean for its final destination, New York City.

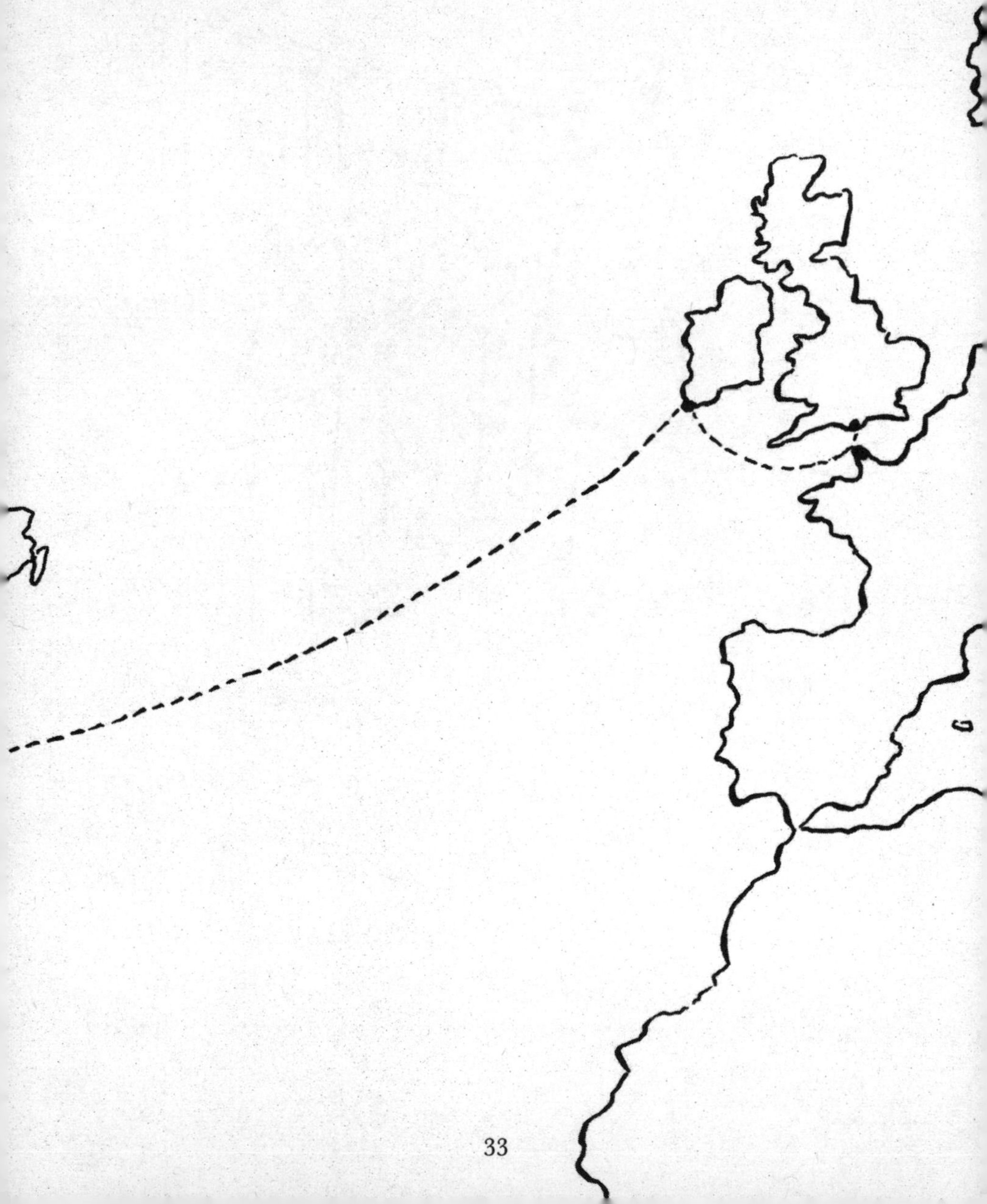

Edward J. Smith was the captain of the *Titanic*'s maiden voyage; he had also conducted its sea trials. Captain Smith had been with White Star Line for more than thirty years and planned to retire after this trip. People called him the "Millionaire's Captain" because he got along so well with rich travelers.

By April 10, Captain Smith and his crew were ready to go. There were more than eight hundred crew members, including engineers, stokers (people who work on furnaces), stewards and stewardesses, chefs, and dishwashers—and also officers who would steer the ship when the captain was otherwise occupied.

The *Titanic's* Grocery List

Before sailing, many supplies had to be loaded onto the ship for the seven-day journey. Among other items, they included:

- 40,000 eggs
- 36,000 oranges
- 8,000 cigars
- 7,000 heads of lettuce
- 2,200 pounds of coffee
- 1,750 quarts of ice cream
- 1,500 gallons of milk

THE VOYAGE BEGINS

The day of *Titanic*'s maiden voyage had arrived. More than thirteen hundred passengers had bought tickets. Most of them were from England; others would get on in France or Ireland.

Thomas Andrews from Harland and Wolff was the first to board. He wanted to check that everything was okay. Then the passengers boarded. Stewards and stewardesses led them to their first-class, second-class, or third-class cabins.

Just before noon, the *Titanic* was ready to cast off. Tugboats tugged it out of its berth as friends, family members, and other well-wishers waved good-bye from the shore. Reporters were also among the crowd, to write about the big event and to take photographs.

The *Titanic* set off for its first stop: Cherbourg, France. It arrived there around dusk, picked up and dropped off passengers, and left at around eight thirty p.m.

The ship reached its second stop—Queenstown, Ireland—around lunchtime the next day. It picked up more than a hundred passengers, mostly Irish emigrants who would stay in the third-class accommodations.

Around two p.m. that day, the *Titanic* headed out into the open seas. It was scheduled to arrive in New York City six days later on April 17.

Famous Passengers

These notable names were among the *Titanic*'s many passengers:

Molly Brown: She was an American actress, activist, and philanthropist (a person who helps others through charitable contributions or work). When the *Titanic* was sinking, she took charge of one of the lifeboats and assisted survivors. In the 1960s, there was a play about her life called *The Unsinkable Molly Brown*, which was made into a film.

John Jacob Astor: The Astors were a wealthy and prominent American family. John Jacob Astor was an inventor, science fiction writer, and businessman who was responsible for building several luxury hotels in New York City, including the Astoria (which today is the Waldorf Astoria) and the St. Regis. He died on the *Titanic*; his wife, Madeleine, who was five months pregnant, survived.

J. Bruce Ismay: He was the chairman of the White Star Line. He was criticized for boarding one of the lifeboats even though the commander of the lifeboat instructed that only women and children be let on. He retired from White Star in 1913

Isidor and Ida Straus:
The Straus family founded
Macy's department store in
New York City. Isidor and
his brother Nathan were
co-owners of Macy's as
of 1896; Isidor also
served in the U.S. House
of Representatives. He
and his wife both died
on the *Titanic*.

Dorothy Gibson: She was an
American silent film actress.
She survived the *Titanic*
disaster and went on to star in
a 1912 film about the incident,
Saved from the Titanic.

LIFE ON BOARD

The first-, second-, and third-class passengers had separate areas to sleep, eat, and recreate. Once on board, they were not supposed to mingle with one another.

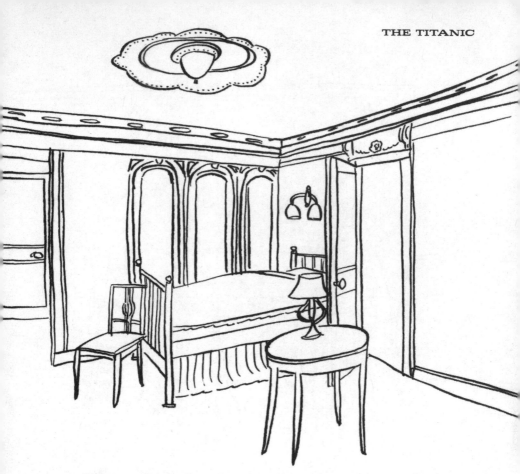

The first-class sleeping accommodations included suites with connecting rooms and were extremely luxurious. The styles of the furniture and decor were from different periods in history. The cheaper cabins with single beds were for the passengers' servants.

The first-class amenities were luxurious too. There were two main restaurants: a large, elegant dining room that could seat more than five hundred diners, and the Café Parisien, which was supposed to look like a sidewalk café in Paris. Dinners were multicourse feasts with the finest wines.

In addition to the restaurants and lounges and other places to relax, there was a heated saltwater swimming pool, a squash court (squash is a game that is played with rackets and a rubber ball), and a gym with state-of-the-art equipment and personal trainers on staff.

The second-class amenities weren't as fancy, but they were still very nice. There was a library for reading and socializing. People played chess, backgammon, and deck games, like ring toss and shuffleboard. The meals they ate in the second-class dining room were almost as good as the meals in first class. Their cabins had mahogany furniture and single beds or bunks.

The third-class amenities were the least fancy of all. The two dining rooms couldn't accommodate everyone at the same time, so people had to eat in shifts. The meals were simple but well made. (The dinner menu on April 14, the *Titanic*'s last night, included roast beef with gravy, sweet corn, boiled potatoes, and plum pudding.)

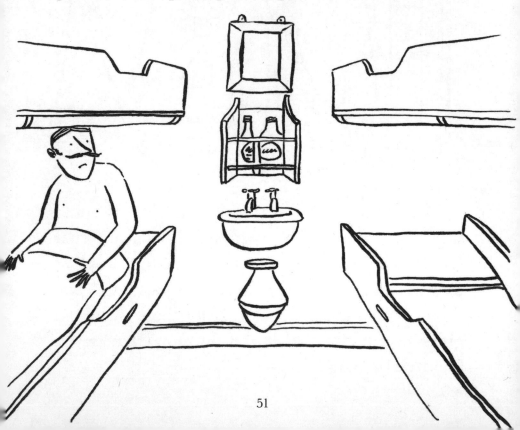

The small, modest cabins in third class could sleep two, four, or six people; this meant that families could stay together, but single travelers had to share quarters. There were two bathtubs—one for the men and boys, the other for the women and girls—that had to be shared by more than seven hundred passengers.

Still, the third-class passengers managed to have a good time. Some of them played musical instruments that they had brought on board. There were lively jump-rope contests and lots of dancing.

In general, all the classes liked to walk along the decks and enjoy the sea air. They also liked to sit on deck chairs to enjoy the view.

THE FIRST WARNINGS

On April 14—four days after leaving Southampton, England—the *Titanic* began receiving warnings about ice and icebergs ahead. The warnings came via wireless radio transmissions from other ships that were in the area. Wireless radiography was a fairly new technology that involved sending and receiving Morse code messages on wireless radios. Two employees of the Marconi Wireless Telegraph Company, Jack Phillips and Harold Bride, manned the *Titanic*'s wireless office for much of its journey.

Captain Smith was apparently not concerned by these warnings; after all, ice and icebergs were common in the northern Atlantic at that time of year. He did make a few changes, like turning the *Titanic*'s course slightly south. He also ordered the men who were watching from the crow's nest to keep an eye out for ice and icebergs. (A crow's nest is a platform at the top of a ship's mast that serves as a lookout area.) But he didn't slow down the ship, which was moving along briskly at around twenty-two knots, which is about twenty-six miles per hour.

Around 9:40 p.m. that night, the wireless office got a message from a ship called the *Mesaba*. It warned of an ice field that included "heavy pack ice" and a "great number" of "large icebergs." But the message never got passed to the *Titanic*'s bridge. (A bridge is the area from where the ship is commanded.)

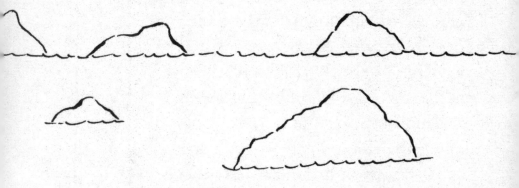

Neither did the next message, which came in at 10:55 p.m. from a nearby ship called the *Californian*. The *Californian* said that it was "stopped and surrounded by ice." Phillips responded: "Shut up, shut up, I am busy."

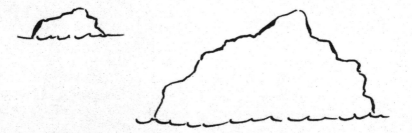

Why didn't the *Titanic*'s wireless office deliver the *Mesaba*'s and *Californian*'s messages to the bridge? One explanation is that the office apparently *was* very busy. It had a huge stack of messages to send from passengers who wanted to write home to friends and families about their exciting sea voyage.

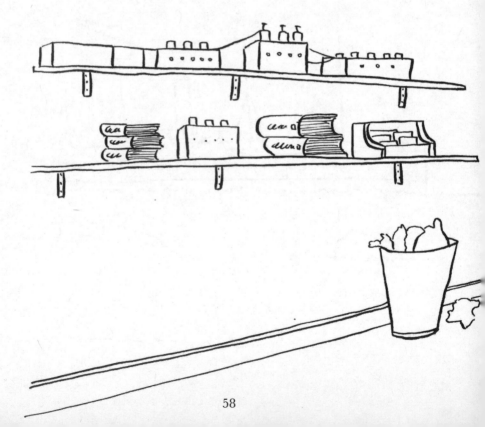

Missing the Boat

Here are some well-known people who missed boarding the *Titanic* for one reason or another:

- Guglielmo Marconi: An Italian inventor and physicist and founder of the company that was responsible for *Titanic*'s wireless equipment.

- Theodore Dreiser: An American novelist.

- Milton S. Hershey: The founder of the Hershey Chocolate Company.

- Three famous (and very wealthy) businessmen also didn't get on the *Titanic*: Alfred Gwynne Vanderbilt, J. Pierpont Morgan, and Henry Clay Frick.

- Ordinary people missed boarding the *Titanic* too. In fact, a few days after the *Titanic* sank, a Michigan newspaper reported the formation of a "Just Missed It" club with 6,904 members!

THE ICEBERG

Captain Smith had gone to his room for the night at around 9:30 p.m. The "officer of the watch"—the person in charge of navigation in the absence of the captain—was First Officer William Murdoch.

At around 11:40 p.m., one of the crow's nest lookouts, Frederick Fleet, spotted an enormous iceberg just ahead. At that point, the *Titanic* was about 460 miles south of Newfoundland, Canada. Fleet rang the bell three times—a signal that something was in the *Titanic*'s path—and also called down to the bridge, which was the standard procedure. In response, First Officer Murdoch ordered the ship to go "hard-a-starboard" (which is a sailing term for "steer hard to the left") and for the engines to be reversed. (Ships don't have brakes, like cars, so this was the only way to try to slow down and stop.)

But the *Titanic* was going too fast to be able to slow down *or* stop in time. At 11:40 p.m., its starboard side collided with the iceberg. Some people on board reported feeling a bump; others said they felt nothing. As the ship continued to move forward,

the iceberg scraped against it with a terrible grating sound.

The iceberg had breached the hull. Water began pouring in.

How Big Was the Iceberg?

The iceberg that collided with the *Titanic* probably started out as a snowflake many thousands of years ago. Over centuries and millennia, it gradually morphed into solid glacial ice. By 1912, its above-water size may have been equal to the size of the Colosseum in Rome.

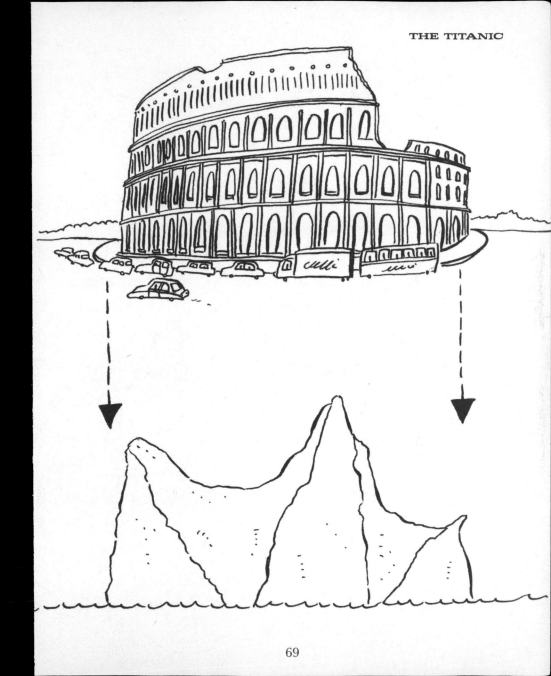

HOPELESS

An important safety feature of the *Titanic* was the fact that the hull was made up of sixteen separate, watertight compartments. The doors between them could be shut remotely from the bridge. That way, if one of the compartments flooded, the water wouldn't spill over into the other compartments.

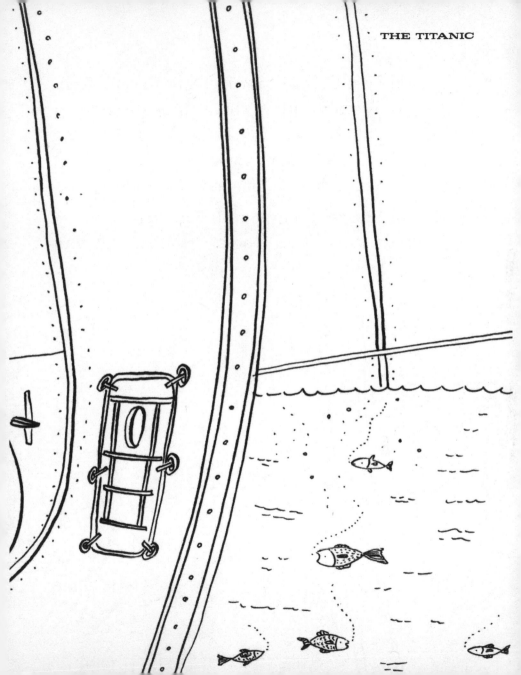

THE TITANIC

When First Officer Murdoch got the call from the crow's nest about the iceberg ahead, he ordered those doors to be shut. But it turned out that the compartments were not watertight after all, and water flowed freely from one to the other.

By this time, Captain Smith had arrived on the bridge and been told about the collision. He and Thomas Andrews, the ship's designer, went below

deck to inspect the damage. When they got there, they discovered that six of the sixteen "watertight" compartments had already been flooded. The maximum the ship could withstand was four; otherwise, it could not stay afloat.

Andrews announced gravely that the situation was hopeless, and that the *Titanic* would sink to the bottom of the ocean in about two hours.

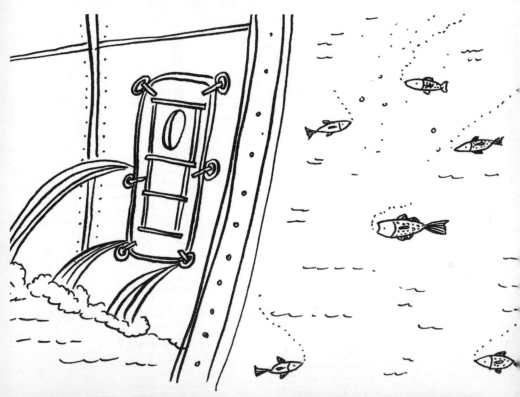

THE DISTRESS SIGNAL

Just after midnight, Captain Smith ordered Jack Phillips and Harold Bride to send out distress signals over the wireless. Several ships answered, including the *Frankfurt* and the White Star Line's *Olympic*, but they were too far away to reach the *Titanic* in time.

The *Carpathia* received the signal too. The Cunard ship, which was about sixty-seven miles to the south, quickly changed course to come to the *Titanic*'s aid.

Strangely, the *Californian*, which had sent the warning message at around 10:55 p.m., never answered. It turned out that its wireless office had closed for the night and never received the *Titanic*'s distress signal.

SOS! CQD!

"SOS" is a common distress signal that can be transmitted by Morse code. Some people think that the letters stand for "Save Our Ship." But actually, they don't stand for anything. Experts chose them because they are easy to transmit and understand in Morse code: three dots, three dashes, and three dots. (Heard through a radio, this would be three short sounds, three long sounds, and three short sounds.)

Another distress signal existed before SOS: CQD. CQ was a general call, or an alert to other radio operators that a message was forthcoming. The D was added to indicate "distress."

When Phillips and Bride sent out the distress signal that fateful night, they used both SOS and CQD.

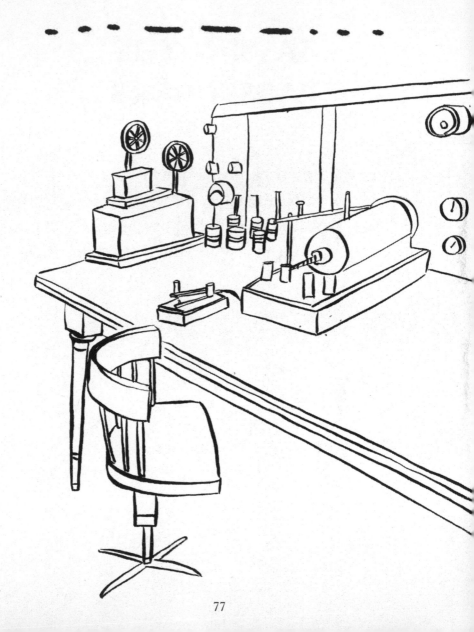

SAVING THE PASSENGERS

An evacuation plan was quickly put into place. Captain Smith instructed his crew to ready the lifeboats. He also ordered the passengers to get into life vests (which were called "life belts" back then).

But many of the passengers didn't take the order seriously. Some continued dining and dancing in their fancy evening clothes. Others remained asleep in their beds.

This all changed when people began to grasp that the *Titanic* was sinking. They hurried toward the lifeboats. Women and children were told to get into them first.

But even this process was confusing and chaotic. Many of the women didn't want to leave their husbands behind. Some of the men tried to board the lifeboats with their wives and children and were told no. Many of the third-class passengers didn't even make it to the lifeboats because they didn't understand English and had no idea what they were supposed to do; also, the third-class deck was the farthest from the lifeboats.

As a result, the first lifeboats that left weren't even half full. This was a huge problem because there had only been twenty lifeboats to begin with, with a total capacity of 1,178. There were more than 2,200 people on the *Titanic*. This meant that almost half of those on the *Titanic* had no way to get off.

Lifeboat Regulations

The twenty lifeboats that the *Titanic* had on board were four more than was required by the regulations. But the *Titanic* actually had enough space to carry at least forty-eight lifeboats.

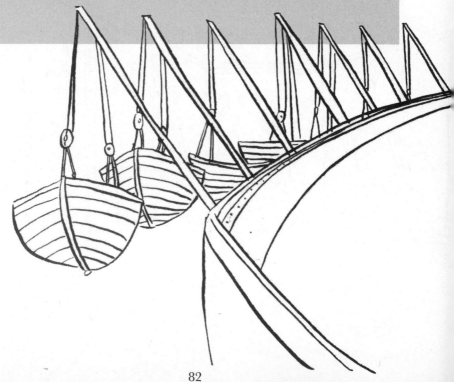

THE SINKING OF
THE *TITANIC*

At around twelve forty-five a.m., the *Titanic* began firing distress flares into the air, hoping to catch the attention of any nearby ships. The *Californian*, which may have been as close as twenty miles away, actually saw the firework-like flares but couldn't figure out where they were coming from.

86

Over the next hour and a half, lifeboats continued being lowered into the icy water—some filled to capacity, some not. As the *Titanic* slowly sank and the dire situation became obvious, more people clamored to get on the lifeboats. Panic ensued.

At approximately two twenty a.m., the *Titanic* disappeared under the surface.

87

The Musicians of the *Titanic*

Eight young musicians had been hired to play music on board the *Titanic*. When the ship began to sink, they left the first-class lounge and moved to the boat deck. They continued to play music in order to help calm and comfort the passengers. Some reports indicate that they didn't stop playing until the very end; all eight men went down with the ship.

90

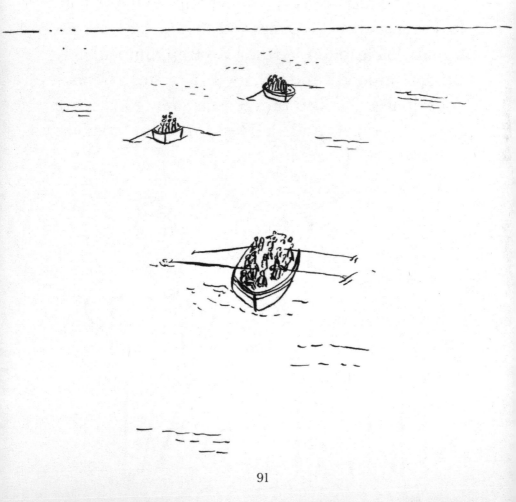

RESCUE

The *Carpathia* was en route from New York City to Europe when they received the *Titanic*'s distress signal. The captain, Arthur Rostron, immediately turned around and headed for the *Titanic*'s coordinates. He also ordered his crew to prepare lifeboats, ropes and ladders, medical stations, blankets, coffee, and hot soup.

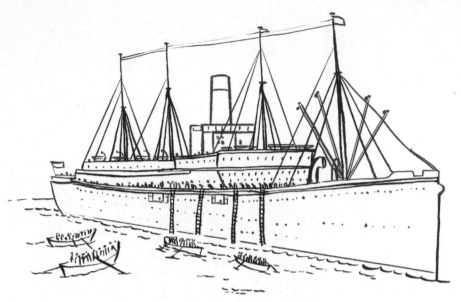

Unfortunately, the *Carpathia* had to travel slowly because of icebergs. At around two forty-five a.m., the crew fired flares so that the lifeboat survivors would know they were coming. The *Carpathia* reached the first lifeboat around four a.m. and started the rescue operation.

The operation took around four hours. In the end, just more than seven hundred people were rescued. Tragically, more than fifteen hundred people had died.

THE AFTERMATH

After all the survivors had been rescued, the *Carpathia* began the somber four-day-long journey back to New York City. A funeral service was held on board for the dead.

The news of the *Titanic* tragedy had spread all over the world. When the *Carpathia* reached New York City, forty-thousand people awaited them.

96

Later, there were many investigations and hearings to find out why the *Titanic* disaster had happened and who was to blame. Captain Smith was criticized for not having slowed the speed of the *Titanic* after hearing about icebergs in the area. A scheduled lifeboat drill had been canceled, which may have contributed to the chaotic dispatching of the lifeboats. Crew as well as passengers were likely confused because a general warning was never sounded. The *Californian* came under heavy fire for not having responded to the *Titanic*'s distress signal and flares, especially since it was only about twenty miles away.

One positive outcome of the terrible event was that safety laws were changed regarding ships and ship travel. Starting in 1913, ships were required to have enough lifeboats to accommodate all passengers on board. Lifeboat drills were mandatory for every voyage. Ships had to keep their radios on and monitored around the clock.

In 1914, the International Ice Patrol was formed to help detect the presence of ice and icebergs in the Arctic and Atlantic Oceans. The organization still exists today and is operated by the United States Coast Guard.

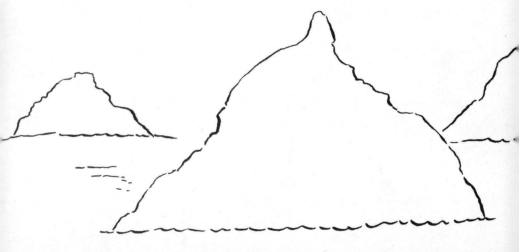

THE DISCOVERY OF THE *TITANIC*

The *Titanic* lay at the bottom of the ocean for seventy-three years, undiscovered. People tried to locate it but were not successful.

All that changed in the summer of 1985. A team led by an American oceanographer named Dr. Robert Ballard was testing a "submersible sled" that could take live images underwater and send them back to a computer monitor. This device, called the *Argo*, went down to the floor of the Atlantic Ocean and sent back images of some old boilers—the *Titanic*'s boilers!

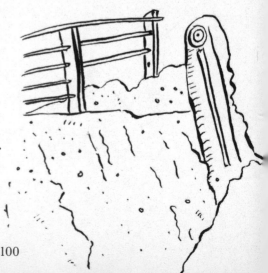

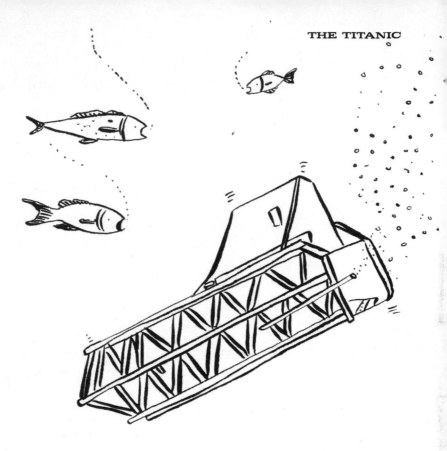

During the following summer, Dr. Ballard and his team returned to that spot with a mini submarine called *Alvin*. They found the *Titanic* two and a half miles below the surface, split in two, along with lots of remains, like furniture and pots and pans.

Since then, many manned and unmanned submersibles have returned to the site to study the *Titanic*'s remains. Theories continue to swirl around about why, exactly, the *Titanic* sank. It was originally believed that the iceberg had caused a single long gash in the hull that had led to the flooding. But no such gash was ever found; instead, scientists detected smaller breaches in the hull and in the seams between the hull plates.

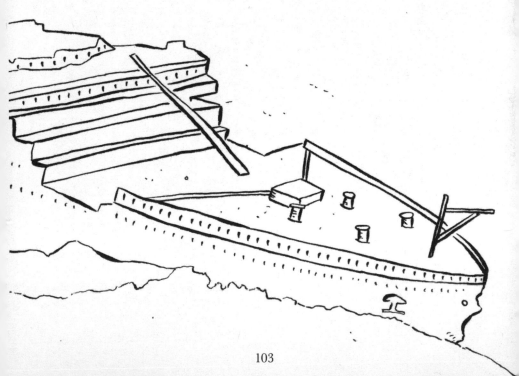

Rusticles

When Dr. Robert Ballard and his team discovered the remains of the *Titanic*, they saw strange formations covering the wreckage. The formations were rust-colored and resembled stalactites. He coined the term "rusticles" to describe them. It was determined that the rusticles were produced by microorganisms that liked to eat rust!

These microorganisms continue to eat away at the rusty *Titanic*. Someday, the ship will cease to exist altogether.

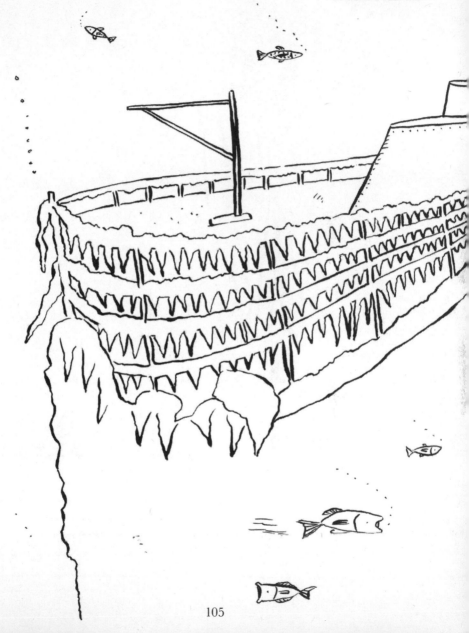

Remembering the *Titanic*

The sinking of the *Titanic* has inspired many books (including books by survivors), as well as several films (such as *A Night to Remember* and *Titanic*). There are many *Titanic* memorials throughout the world, like the *Titanic* Memorial Lighthouse and Straus Park in New York City, and the Women's *Titanic* Memorial in Washington, D.C. There are memorials in Great Britain, Ireland, Canada, and Australia, as well.

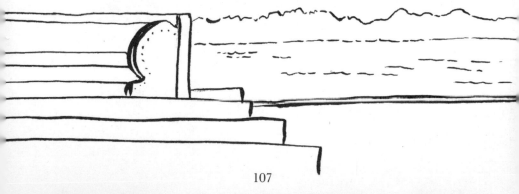

Well, it's been a great adventure. Good-bye, Titanic!

Where to next?

Also available:

Selected Bibliography

BBC UK Online, http://www.bbc.co.uk/history/topics/iceberg_sank_titanic and
http://www.bbc.co.uk/history/topics/belfast_golden_age_shipbuilding#p00qjppf

Discovery Online, http://news.discovery.com/tech/titanic-wireless-120411.htm

Encyclopedia Britannica Kids Online, www.kids.britannica.com

Encyclopedia Britannica Online, www.britannica.com

National Geographic Online, http://channel.nationalgeographic.com/titanic-100-years/articles/life-on-board-recreation/

National Museums Northern Ireland Online, www.nmni.com

The Smithsonian Online, http://www.smithsonianmag.com/ist/?next=/history/seven-famous-people-who-missed-the-titanic-101902418/

NANCY OHLIN is the author of the YA novels *Always, Forever* and *Beauty* as well as the early chapter book series Greetings from Somewhere under the pseudonym Harper Paris. She lives in Ithaca, New York, with her husband, their two kids, four cats, and assorted animals who happen to show up at their door. Visit her online at nancyohlin.com.

ADAM LARKUM is a freelance illustrator based in the United Kingdom. In his fifteen years of illustrating, he's worked on more than forty books. In addition to his illustration work, he also dabbles in animation and develops characters for television.

BLAST BACK!